Ghazzali's

Treasure

Chest

Written by
Ghazzali
(Jason Kimble)

Dedication

No one has shown so greatly and explained so perfectly the glory of our Creator's divine compassion for us, and the whole of His creation, than what has been witnessed in the loving souls of our own mothers. When our blessed Creator issued forth His divine decree to fashion such remarkable women, by imbuing them with incomparable qualities such as unquenchable and unconditional love. It indeed testified to being a divine act from a loving and wise God.

I believe there is "Hidden Wisdom" that resonates within the soul of a mother that relates to us the most essential quality regarding God's nature. That being the sovereign virtue of love. This extraordinary vessel that God has chosen to teach us such compassion, through a nurturing spirit that critically shapes who we are and what we are destined to become. Many of us stand in complete amazement of this extraordinary vessel. This great womb of mercy from which we were sprung; and thus we cherish the women that bore us, we cherish more so the Creator who anointed her (Mom). The first of all life's tender experiences has been enjoined upon her!   This raiment of hers is a crown divinely appointed to her. Infallibly assigned to the loving nature and natural strength that is hers.

Are we even aware of how her face, always radiating, full of love and acceptance, creates parallel expressions upon ours? As we are totally smitten with delight, our eyes dancing in excitement. She is the first to stir our emotional energies by putting laughter in our hearts. She is the first to assure, and bequeath an untold wealth of security in our emotions. Her tender embraces created a thirst for love's most affectionate offerings. A thirst in of itself that can be equated to the very hunger initiated at her breast.

Moving 'generally' to 'specifically' to the one my heart has fastened upon. Visualized so vividly every detail and contour that makes up her face that it requires no portrait. Her image is burned forever on my mind. A regal inscription upon my mental composition.
I have seen many revelations in you, my dearest Queen Victoria. Revelations unveiled tactfully and carefully that would be life sustaining as it prepared me for future events in my life that I would encounter. Revelations capable of developing character. You have granted me without question, one of God's greatest gifts ... Love.

For all of life's great lessons that God was impressing upon my conscience were rooted in the many conversations I had with you (my mother) God's chosen vessel.

My dear Queen, my dilemma is my inability to express the depth of my gratitude beyond these walls. My soul has struggled to come up with more ennobling demonstrations to share this new profound epiphany of love and gratitude.

It's increasingly difficult to express the fullness of this new found sense of gratitude and appreciation for all of your noteworthy actions and intentions. Knowing that all of my earnest toiling will be insufficient to meet the standard of love in which you have provided.

Within this Treasure Chest collection ... this precious diamond forged with life's hard lessons, nuggets of wisdom, born from gem-full truths that have all been inspired and originated with you in mind.

The origins of my soul's first taste of wisdom began by way of those sweet and sober words falling from a tongue full of Grace! So, here's how they have been purged, formed, and conceptualized in my mind, compounded by the struggles, trials, joys, and sorrows known to our experiences as Mother and Son! Now they have become the pulse by which my heart determines its truths. Living by them, choosing what is most wise and making decisions "befitting" of the Creator's purpose for my life has always been your dearest aspiration for me. As you open this Treasure Chest and witness what is in your son's Heart, it is my hope that whatever beauty you find, is an eternal reflection of what is within your own.

Flesh of My Flesh
Bone of My Bones

Forever Yielding In Honor of You
Queen Victoria, Your Son, Ghazzali.

Foreword by
Randy G. George

Growing up I would often escape my
humble surroundings into a glorious
world of fantasy. In my mental
wanderings I would often find myself the
sole heir of an unknown, distant relative
leaving me an incredible sum of money.
I would imagine receiving a phone call or
an official letter informing me of my
fortunate position.
My…how things would change for me, I
would no longer want for anything. I
would be prosperous and famous. I
would enjoy great security and power.
But more than anything else I would be
important, popular. and interesting. I

would be the most sought after boy by all the cute girls.

My family would also enjoy the fruits of my new found riches, especially mom, my queen. If anyone deserved to be elevated to an enviable position, it was my mom.

Every child at one time or another has fled to their own fanciful world. A world in which all is right and they themselves are the omnipotent center. It is part of being a child.

Also part of being a child is not fully understanding what we seek. As a child, I envisioned money helping me obtain a wealth of stuff. Yet, I was unable to realize that money could not make me a better person. It could not guarantee me success, popularity, or give me lasting relationships. In short, it could not secure for me a fulfilled existence.

Children actually want to live, be happy, grow, and triumph. It is the hunger of the human heart. The compulsion that exist in them is the longing in the hearts of all, to live, laugh, love, learn, and lead their own lives But they discover early in life that life can be frightening and overwhelming. It is filled with difficulties and obstacles that can utterly try us. As they encounter these things they experience a sense of vulnerability and uncertainty. With this reality comes the temptation to escape into fantasy, which they often do. It's nothing more than a shield from these frightening feelings.

So they dream, as I did, of creating for themselves a world that will promote and protect them. Little knowing that there is a greater and more enduring resource in life. One that cannot be procured by money, but can itself generate and guarantee money.

What is this most prized resource?

W-I-S-D-O-M

Wisdom is a precious and invaluable commodity. Unlike material wealth, when used properly, wisdom can afford us character, inner peace, and a fulfilled existence. As one of the wisest men who ever lived wrote, "Happy is the person who finds wisdom. Her merchandise is better than silver and her gain more than fine gold. She is more precious than rubies, and all the things that one may find cannot be compared to her: Her ways are ways of pleasantness and all her paths are peace. Forsake her not and she shall preserve you. Love her and she shall keep you. Exalt her and she shall promote you. She shall bring you to honor if you embrace her. " Children do not understand the value of wisdom (Especially, applied wisdom) which is the principle aim of knowledge and instruction to cultivate in us a capacity for discernment and the intelligent application of knowledge. To be truly wise (mature) is to use knowledge well.

Let us notice the compensation of wisdom: Happiness, security, peace, promotion, honor, pleasant ways, and peaceful paths. The latter being the result of sound judgment. Doesn't that sound ideal and desirable? Doesn't it arouse new interest in our quest for strategies to conquer and to succeed, to be secure and fulfilled?

Wisdom is all around us. The ear that learns to hear shall dwell among the wise. For they love their souls. As children we had the luxury of having people to care for us. Some of these care takers did better than others, and if you're reading this, we made it. These caregivers provided substance for us in many forms. But I believe the greatest gift was their words of wisdom... Their insight. For me, like Ghazzali, it was my mother. For you it could have been someone else. Whomever it was, their contribution cannot be overstated. Unfortunately many of those lessons we didn't understand then as we struggled to make sense of our inner and outer worlds.

Hopefully today we do.

Hopefully, today we understand the value of wisdom over money.

Hopefully, we've discovered that material wealth may buy many tangibles but it cannot buy the intangibles such as love, peace, character, life, etc. Hopefully, we realize the magical and narrow minded way we viewed money as access into a happy life pales in comparison to the life carved and lived in adulthood through rightly executed wisdom. Hopefully, we have a deep understanding that wisdom truly promotes us into a life extraordinarily better than that of material wealth.

I believe Ghazzali has learned the value of wisdom. I believe the wealth of wisdom his mother stored in his heart has at last seized him and consequently elevates him. I recommend you sit with him as I have been privileged to do so, and hear the wisdom abounding in his heart. I believe you will be enriched and empowered. Surely you will have the inheritance you sought for as a child.

Forward

Dear reader, the nugget before each quote represents the original order in which this humble body of work was compiled.
This is intended to give the reader the truest feel of the author's original process in writing this book, and how our minds naturally shift from one theme to the next.

Chapter One

Cold Steel

"For the life of me, I don't know what has gotten into you or what has happened. And I refuse to lose you to these streets. But you have chosen a path , and God knows I have prayed that whatever is needed for you to return to what He has called you to do, then do it. No matter the severity, just give me the strength to bear it."

-Ghazzali's Mother

Wherever isolation and unflinching reality meets, the conscience speaks.

This time around, listening will not be an option.

Confinement

164

Prison is so overcrowded. A socially congested institution with determined minds showing a menacing behavior that willfully undermines social order or civil law. Due to whatever psychological or emotional imbalances that lay under the layers of such criminality, there are rare displays of civility being shown between inmates that's truly sincere in nature. This massive institution with its unique breed of dangerous minds are forming with greater stimulus, being shaped by more stranger imaginations for barbarism. Often enough, I wonder why such little bloodshed has taken place.

64

Simply, the prisoner's struggle is no more than his belief or non-belief in his own redeeming value.

67

The prisoner's most valued lesson for the survival of his incarceration, is the success of his own life. Therefore, to learn daily the art of living is only to be found in the quality of his own thoughts. Without this lesson being learned vigilantly, his rescinding into whatever evil hole he may desire to emerge from will be inevitable, and therefore his permanent resting place.

66

Enshrouded in the blackest of night, there can be seen the dancing silhouette of the prisoner's pen, speaking volumes about his most sought after ambitions. Therein, lies the heart's dearest concerns.

122

The prisoner's 'hole' of opportunity is liken unto a rat hole. An undetectable crevice, plunge into the darkest corners, requiring no erect vertebrae of human dignity for its passing. Those who seek to afford us such passing requires total abject humiliations. Oh, what it is to have fallen upon such crushing times!

69

The real "crisis" within our prison population is to be an observer of GROWN undefined men, being forced to learn what it is to be civil to one another. When knowing who you are is the most dignifying act to one's own self, it is the basis of what one contributes and learns to give to others.

98

As we witness the darkest days of human affairs become more obviously darkened by the minute, the search continues to find significance in any form, And this, to a world that seemingly has turned a deaf ear to basic human needs and the cry of the innocent. Then, imagine the strife that submerges us (PRISONERS) here. The most meager mundane acts of life take on a grave importance. That easily one's life can be snuffed out on the most frivolous menial matters. For here, everything in every way represents one's self-image and masculinity. A most unsettling cry for importance (by any means) proceed with due caution. Hell, am I not still describing our global human family?

144

It is just too tight of a desperate world, to show that "here" I'm searching tirelessly to find 'IT' in us. It's hard. The rule is ... everyone's own woes comes first, second, and third. Literally, THIS IS ALL IT IS! SUCK IT UP. I hate to step on and over you but compassion shown cost too much! You know…It's to a great extreme what one does to weigh in heavily on the "Manly scale".   "Here" sincerely hurting one another comes in all various forms. When every underline statement is to declare "WHO YOU ARE NOT –VS- WHO THEY ARE"!

142

The constrain, constricted, and uneventful routine of incarceration will place an enormous demand on the human mind to become more sound in critical thinking.   Many ennobling reasons truly do exist. Like… Encouraging us in this endeavor.   Though we all have found no better pressing motive for ourselves than for our own sanity.   The challenge is either sink or swim!

65

To act consistently upon the noble urge to rise above the consequences and the degradation of our own crippling choices, defines the real meaning of will power.

145

One of the most sought after hidden treasures with much diligence which can be obtained in the stillness of these walls, is the 'freedom' to examine thoroughly one's currently held beliefs. Yes, to do this without the bombardment of so called 'free' society. Propaganda coming through various media outlets is an occasion of great joy. Way to often these outlets are filled with ideological agendas, initiatives and subliminal pro- actions that keeps one suppressed in discovering his or her own thoughts. Oh, what it is to witness a mass slaughtering of minds!

86

Ah, who so want to hear the crying details of a sordid life entrapped in cold walls .... No one! What 'meaningful' interest should the world hold towards us here. So the 'Tales' of prisoners remain untold, stories unknown, and largely unwanted. Yet, if this was true of us, I would be content to cease with this madness. But sadly, there are many more (hold-in cells) among free society, than there could ever be among us here. It is ultimately unto these caged in prisoners that the world with its preoccupation within itself has failed to listen! Why refuse to listen to the affairs of your own heartbeat?

Choices

70

Life, choices, and its yielding consequences and results. The ultimate lasting 'outcome' of all our choices is the home that we have created for ourselves within our souls. To examine the quality of this home, let us simply ask, how well does your conscience sleep in the bed of its solitude?

Change

13

Change isn't just about moving forward. It involves moving upward. More than the overall alteration of conditions from one state to another. Though this is largely preferred by most, yet poignantly life's call for change is usually not in the alteration of the condition themselves, but in the way they was once held, viewed, or perceived.

47

Be not of those who shuns the truth regarding themselves when presented, in due season mockery of what you could have been produces the greatest sense of shame.

1

When looking at the prospects and possibility of real social change, I have only encountered two mental positions or outlooks taken fully. The first primarily being the all-consuming role of leadership we largely desire others to play or assume. Then secondly of the two, which is most critical, is the role that we see ourselves having assumed or at least making an earnest attempt to. Consequently, the former is the majority position commonly taken, and because of such social change remain ideally disputed about than concretely pursued. Leaving the latter position overwhelmed with the enormity of its task, doubtful, in its outcome and suspicious of others commitment. Eventually, even their own.

5

In keen observation to the 'nature' of change, we have unfortunately defined 'resistance' as an enemy to change. When in fact, it is essentially the most delicate part of its process.   In order for something to 'become' or to 'be', this dynamic of friction or tension is always required.   Therefore, I have sought to have a wiser resolve to acknowledge 'resistance' not as some arch-nemesis to change, but as the key catalyst.

200

Likened to all social institutions that seek to foster a redemptive program for transformation in human consciousness and behavior, the prisoner's reformation process must always begin with a thorough in-search, and a willingness to have right understanding of one's own life and rightful interpretation of one's own experience. In this most intimate, immediate task, most men will fail.

Freedom

87

The just cry of the rebel isn't really against the notion of the law itself. It is against the 'principle' sentiment that undergirds it, that says I'm unmindful and unheedful of your social dilemma.

121

True revolution is litigation by force. In these times diplomacy becomes more shrewdly tactful in negotiating, not with an outstretched hand but with an iron fist.

114

The liberality of any action is unto each man's own conscience. And though that same action can become of form of bondage to another, it's   better to indulge innocently in one's own error than to woefully engage in the sphere of another man's sense of right for the sense of peace he will share. For when the heat of suffering shall consume him for the betterment of adhering to his principle of truth, such peace will truly escape you! You will not find such peace abiding within you, and such heat of suffering will lay slain to those who have been false to their own convictions.

120

Grave humiliation marks the road to freedom, but the superficiality of honors and dignities of privilege from the oppressor are great signpost of its detour.

Underlying Realities

184

One betrays the good works of his own hands by way of bad character. It's much easier for people to remember the idea of who they think you are than what they know you have actually accomplished.

127

The real game of life, is the war for the human mind.

171

For any ethnicity to truly win ... To be a national force with identity, culture, prominent language, or powers of structure, they must become their own builders, shapers, and developers of their own mind. This entails central beliefs of a person to political paradigms and world views that will be shared as a whole. They must be the founding fathers of their own institutional learning centers, from which intellectual development and training will take place and form. This means creators and arrangers of the assembled information, along with developers of the basis policy and curriculum, not just passionate conveyors of these lessons. Dictators of the subjects, and fierce evaluators of the authenticity of what's been assembled and innovators of the system of how it's being dispensed.

154

Life seems to be a great moral challenge, to be authentically who you are in all things, and to search for the authenticity in everything you do.

175

If one is to know the comfort and joy of life, he must seek it first within his own self! This being true, one is most certainly compelled then to focus one's mind in one ennobling absolute consecrated direction. Removing all doubts and suspicions for that which he's earnestly seeking ... upon journeying this course there awaits a beautiful shoreline for him to embark upon. Where there's an ocean of timeless thoughts that most consoling, pure, and serene. Never to be known in mere places, objects, or even persons.

The measured value of any choice is determined by its long term results. Yet its merit is weighed by the moral goodness that lies within. The best choice is always the morally correct one. For us humans the problem is not knowing the morally correct one, but accepting wholeheartedly that it is.

178

The curse of free-will is that there is always an undeniable cost.

179

Every meaningful decision in life is made in the dark (private corners of our minds), yet only the searchlight of our conscience will determine if it's worthy to be displayed or not.

180

Warring with a man's right to chose is like questioning one's right to exist. We naturally accept his right to exist by the simple fact he does ... it's a non-negotiable matter indeed. So it should be when it comes to men choosing what they chose and how they chose. If not, dear friend, you will be forever bewildered by man and his choices. Even more at greater lost concerning your own.

Responsibility and Discipline

181

Responsibility is essentially objectivity, management, discipline, and lastly good character. Anything else that can be added will show itself in due season.

182

Fundamentally vital for any man psyche is to know that he has four chief obligations in which his whole life will be based. That is the obligation to oneself, family, community, and the world at large. However, if he's grossly ignorant or severely mismanage the first two, then latter two will experience the devastating repercussions thereof. That being the community that surrounds him and the world at large.

183

Show me a man who lays claims to have eaten this dish until his full, and I will show you a man who doesn't essentially understands his need of it. And therefore, hasn't been beaten enough by the bitter end of its stick. The stick of discipline.

184

Responsibility is the spine that makes a man a man. And irresponsibleness is a cancer to his bones. This cancer is the spirit of laziness and absent- mindedness. Consequently, it's only cure is the iron rod of discipline and mental vigilance.

185

The fear of being held highly accountable makes cowards out of many thirsty ambitious men. Thus making them most negligent towards their rightful duties that's attach to such an ambitions. Yet, I remind you that their negligence isn't due to their lack of desire for the success or what they are longing for, but the unwillingness to bear the consequences for when they fall short.

186

The target of life is success, and the various means by which to achieve it's arrows. Then the bow itself by which arrow's placed, made steady, carefully aimed, and lastly launched is none other than discipline.

Chapter Two

Warring Within

"Son, life is choice-driven. Life is the outcome of the choices that you are making. You must humble yourself and listen. Pride goes before a fall, a haughty spirit before destruction."

-Ghazzali's Mother

There is no neutrality or neutral ground in this struggle called life. Every moment you are defining who you are, deciding who you will be, and determining what you were destined to become.

Self-identity

14

Truth by its nature is confrontational.
Falsehood deceives by way of
flattery... Falsehood grant us
permission to remain as we are, truth
empowers us to be as we should.

2

All human struggles begin and end
here. The fight for identity is to
know the real power of what it means
to define oneself. The world is
caught somewhere in between. For
what we project to the world is
understood to be who we are saying
we are, rather than this supposed
Self-Definition is largely our own
creation or your acceptance of an

identity determined by external factors.   Either way, to the world it matters not. It's only concern is will we benefit or suffer because of it.

Sin

🪨 18

To sin, is an act (deed or thought) that disrobe man of his highest state of being. Of him being clothed in the prestigious apparel of pure enlightened and joy-filled rationality. To have disembarked from this divinely prescribed throne of dignity that has been set before us, is to have chosen to live in the squalor of depraved ignorance.

🪨 16

Sin, essentially is impaired reasoning...A faltering in producing, seeking, maintaining, and

having ennobling intentions, or
being governed by divinely inspired
thoughts.

48
When potential leaks out, rejoice not,
in what it has shown, but glory in
what remains hidden and has yet to
be revealed.

188
Once the path of self-actualization
has begun, man's own soul will
experience a profoundly silent unrest.
This shall remain until 'all' that is
'true' of himself is fully discovered,
known, and truly experience.   This
sort of human progress will (always)
be the hallmark of our universe.

116
The essence of all human struggle
towards it's own nobility, is to

simply eradicate some form of 'identified' human suffering. Either that which has been self-imposed or caused by outside forces.

150

This may be a terrible strange sound in our human ears that violence can easily ensnare any individual. The difficulty may lay largely with the wrestling belief of its execution, but its sentiment is seemingly readily with us. When prevented with a prolong blockade between ourselves and our most dearly cherished possessions, it matters not, if the desired object is tangible or intangible. Has not history proven the worst of violence employed by humans has been some romanticized, fantastical, and intoxicating idea. Because then it's not what your hand can unjustly grasp, but of what your mind perceives, it has the right to believe.

181

I present the simplest idealism of life. That is a pursuit of happiness that simply doesn't destroys a person's soul in the process. The oddity is that this has become wickedly complicated for the human. By this being on a vast alarming global state, I reckon that greater lines of thoughts towards such 'simple idealism' must emerge. Something more expansive, inclusive, and of a wide range that permeates with the collective humanity in mind. But who will sacrifice to some real degree their own regarded sacred interest of its group's ideas of how the pursuit of happiness should be pursued? The sacrifice seems too great, when innumerable identities, roles, and whole livelihoods has been formed

and shaped. Thereby, I say to our
great dismay, war will be ensuing us
even more. Whereas, being truly
human will become the new
endangered species.

147
High aspirations, but lower
preparations, has made nightmares
out of plenty dreams.

128
The disheartening reality of our
human fragility is found in us, feeling
what we do, when we absolutely
shouldn't.   Then us 'not' feeling as
we ought, when we absolutely
should.

148
The world has become so loveless ...
where the lovelessness abounds,
lawlessness will reign even more.

Such lawlessness will consume us with gross appearance. The order of the day, is to seek yours first, then it's "wherever the chips may fall after that", "my pursuit in life is entirely for me and mine. What a spirit to describe such an advancing age." This, "I got to have it" at all cost. This all consuming need to posses something or someone is mightily great in our lustful minds, is it not? One may dare ask, "Aren't we all after something?" I do reckon mightily so. Yes I believe in all our striving, let it be to become fully in possession of one's own self. Wouldn't you think? Name a mightier, sweeter, lovelier possession as this? In such a state of being, one is very whole, and putting others in the equations as you think of yourself becomes a native air that we all can enjoy to breathe.

192

What is human maturity?
Except to think well, consistently, to show benevolence in all things, to speak circumspectly, without forethought of causing injury, to have firm resolve in one's own convictions, and to retire in the solace of one's conscience to simply do better than yesterday.

Spiritual Harms and Dangers

198

I'm of the opinion that a soul needs only to cling steadfastly to one evil for his feet to enter the door of many others.

197

To live beneath the standard of whom you are and your own acknowledged self-worth, is to single-handedly become the villain behind your own victimization.

38

A mind void of meaningful occupation is a sure company of annoyance to anyone and everyone even at a distance.

39

A mind that is constant in thinking only subjectively with regard to its own emotion, is naturally subdued by them. Therefore he is a tornado in human form. Stay clear of its path.

88

Eyes sealed with endless darkness due to hopelessness, leads to vindictiveness and a perverse churning within the soul; an appetite for a gross savagery, to feast tirelessly on anything that satisfies its hunger for damnation. Any act of flashing human sensibilities is camouflage. A man who doesn't believes in the certainty of hope's promises, is a species of another kind, the habitat of the living is no longer suitable for him.

26

Beware of false dreams! They are the ideal things we imagine the most about or think about at the back of our minds. Though our hands bear no signs of toiling in the labor force of this world (where) that which we have richly imagine must materialize. This testifies that our dreams were not really anchored in a heart of faith. Which always energizes the will to labor relentlessly and to be resilient after the images deep within us. He who fails to make perfect his labor, foolishly waits for a harvest that will never come.

19

To know a sense of loneliness is truly
human, but to be alone and know not
how to keep company with oneself,
is the beginning process of becoming
alienated and inhumane.

53

The grotesque arrogance of man has
never ceased to amaze me.
Watching us with this seething
rebellious spirit that seeks to find all
sorts of 'pseudo' intellectual notions
to avoid life's most simplest truth.
That is 'he' (man) is miserable
insufficient to be an infallible source
of guidance of his own life course
and direction. Humility is simply
the genuine admittance that we are in
need of help and that we have ready
our spirits to follow suit.

71

The naivety of being young, the staunch arrogance of immaturity seems often to walk hand in hand. It is both the sincerity they have in the belief that the world around them will fail without them, or that because of them the world has all of sudden found meaning.

131

A man who believes by practicing religious rituals that spiritual ascent is possible while being steadily unheedful to the divine laws (such as love, truth, humility, etc) in which all ritualistic performances signifies, embodies, and seeks to convey, is one to be truly saddened by. For whatever language of heaven he desires to ascend will only remain echoing sounds vibrating in one's own head.

180

Beware of the lowly whisper, the
decadent call, the alluring gesture,
the primitive flame, that swaggering
command that says of us pure
indulgence ...Eat, drink, be merry,
Take thy fill ...just because.
For anything that has such sentiment
is very instinctively primitive. But
surely there still exist within an
higher level of normal consciousness
that entails a shaping of sound,
sobering thoughts having a creative
power to incite passions for
righteousness living. Showing us that
this form of beauty is an inherit trait
of the human soul… just as well is
instinctive, yet very divine

106

To exert oneself for a certain position
may show initiative, yet in return

one's performance may be subjected to more scrutiny and speculation. But to be called upon, seems far much better, having graciously and dutifully accepted. So, then if misfortunes or mishaps befall you in fulfilling duties required, one may find true sympathy. Even at its worse, there will still linger an apologetic sense of possibly having been misplaced not mistrust. But to those being too anxious, overly assertive, upon such times you may be subjected not just to having your performance criticized. But your intentions questioned and much discussed about in hidden places.

56

As unveiling greatness becomes disclosed, the temptation for a greater capacity of evil just as well becomes apparent.

187
To suffer for the lack of knowledge is one thing, but to suffer for the lack of desiring it is another.

188
The real bankruptcy of life is to drop your bucket in the well of your spirit, thirsty for spiritual substance and virtue, and then afterwards to come up empty.

189
To be found loveless in life is not about finding one to love or your lack of ability to love but you coming to believe there is none worthy to be the recipient of it, even yourself.

190

Sit with a man, he'll tell you his thoughts. Stand with a man, he'll display his convictions. Walk with a man, he'll explain his ways.
Run with a man, he'll express his fears. Sleep alongside of a man, he'll paint his dreams. Live with man, he'll manifest his character.
Die beside him, you'll understand why he lived!

191

Ever seen a man deeply starving while watching others around him eating ... as he wonders to himself: Do they know my plight? Do they feel obligated to share what they have? Do they think my condition is by way of my own choosing ? Or even more...Did they design this for their own amusement and my humiliation?

The thin line between this complex
logic and this delusional view!
Yet, this is the image that comes to
mind as I watch our youth react to the
injustices within their own society.
Is their starvation by their own hands
or by some great design? Or the
complex combination of both?

192
Every day your life preaches a
sermon. Every circumstance becomes
a part of the scripture, every response
becomes a verse, your every action
therefore determines its meanings,
and the affect it has on everyone else
determines the truth of your salvation
or damnation. Therefore what kind of
sermon are you?

193

The poverty of the mind is the iron
chain that binds the oppressed to the
oppressor. The poverty of the spirit is
what keeps the oppressor under the
yoke of the oppressed, and strangely
enough both are in need of each other
for their liberation.

194

The true secrets of a sage is not found
in the wisdom he speaks,   but in the
spirit of his heart which determines
how he listen to those around him.

195

Of all tales that are to be written,
none is greater than the tale of death.
For even the tale of life doesn't know
the ending to its own story. For the
mysterious tale of death keeps all of
its secrets...Therefore, may it be as
gracious to you as I pray it unto me ...

For all anyone can do is to live well
and hope for the best.

196

The purest speech among men are of
those who intends well when they
speak, reason well when it's spoken,
applied well when they finish, and
glory not in the affect among others
when they leave. So then we haven't
heard pure speech since days of the
prophets.

197

The greatest shame of any lie is that
the teller begins to believe that it's
true and those who knows it's a lie
find reasons for it to be believe as
true.

Chapter Three

The Dawn

"You see how well I did today"?
 Listen son, I'm proud of you. But
remember it was God using you as a
vessel, as a channel to bless the lives of
others. You are gifted, have been
anointed, for a great work and great
things."
"Mom, you are constantly ignoring how
much preparing and work I had to put
into it".
 "Yeah, baby I know, I witness it, but
Jason it's still 'His work' being done
through you. Don't ever forget that."

-Ghazzali's Mother

"To see the light as it illuminates the reality of all things around you, only being entranced by your own dark silhouette is the curse of life. Upon the shoulders of the unheedful spirit lays the heavy burden of shame. The path that lies ahead, though enshrouded by great silence, is filled with volumes of mockery and humiliation.

Prayer

9

Prayer is relational in nature, just like all relationships it is built one conversation at a time. So it is with the divine, as we have witnessed in our speaking intimately with each other, we often times leave wondering if we were really heard, or understood… Even with all such complexities, we know we are still bound for yet another one.

42

What physical labor is to the body and what studying is to the intellect, so prayer and meditation is to the spirit ...

10

Prayer is in every sense a discipline of a most strenuous nature. It is centering the soul in the presence of the divine, which is the root of our soul's origin, being the essence from which it comes. Thus remain faithful until we sense the presence of divinity not only from without, yet even more from within.

11

Since prayer is centering the soul, so centering is a disciplined art. Whatever is an art is a skill. A skill is a gift developed. This becomes forming of a habit, a habit becomes a continuum of life, and so it must be said of prayer. Prayer is a divine continuum of human existence.

118
If one can remember that prayer should be the natural instinctive language of one's own heart, therein sincerity shall never be amiss

Faith

113
"Belief is simply the eyes of the human soul."

105
No one is firm in anything without the power of conviction. For that power establishes us concretely in our pattern of behavior, keeping us unrelenting in our pursuits, and secure in who we are. Find one who is unshakable in what they

believe, and there lies a solid heart, well-contented, and built for tough times.

166
Rich similarities exist between faith and the natural force we called wind. Both are unseen, subtle, mysteriously gracious, and yet fierce ... spiraling, elevating, critically questionable of its directing objective, then all of sudden seriously fleeting.   Faith and the wind are powerfully affecting, effecting, continually giving substance and animation to life's most tangible realities that are working to shape our world.

17
The pinnacle of faith is 'seeing' with the heart. The hidden hand (which itself is not caused) that causes life to posses the realities it does. Yet not requiring of our physical eyes constant tangible manifestations for its confirmation.

114

Faith is the root of salvation and good
deeds are its fruits ... For was not
salvation(eternal life) symbolically
represented as the "Tree of Life"

195

When intelligence, reaching its end,
arriving upon the shoreline of depleted
rationality, only then, does this miracle
walk of faith truly begin. Yes, crossing
our ocean-like minds, where we are
spent swimming, drowning, in its
mysteries over to the divine.

24

In our struggle of upward mobility
towards our blessed creator, it seems all
hang in the balance between faith and
reason, which feels to be like polar
opposites at times. The intensity of
such moves toward one that is infinite,

both faith and reason, have been instrumental. At times it seems faith will never lead me where my reasoning can't adjust for all things to be most practical. Then at times, yet reasoning seems to reach bridges that needed to be crossed and its (reasoning) own strength to carry me over became miserably waning. As a result the greater things of divinity, stood most obscure. There, faith stood most welcoming to the challenge, crossing over what seemingly was incapable of such crossing. Miraculously enough, faith crosses me over. In the after-glow of such crossing, faith begins to teach reasoning, what was once incomprehensible ... Imagine that...

83

There is lurking in every human, a human personage, a fixture, super character, there is yet to be attained by many of others. Presently our hands constantly yield things that betray it immensely so if I was to speak now of this 'character ambition', my talk among men will make me that of a fool but equally, wretchedly confounding is to remain silent to my own heart's cry, thus validating their claim ... So I stand, without question waiting to be heard!

Consciousness

96

We must continue to fight mentally with one another, we must challenge each other intellectually, we must confront each other in our logic, until we cease to sense any stimuli to formulate beliefs, attitudes or norms that have no objectivity, until we are left with a well-defined aim when it comes to dealing with undeniable reality!

15

There is no true state of consciousness ever attained without working thoroughly (truly) through the process of what it will prescribe and demand of the "conscience" to remain free and unimpaired!

Wisdom

141

Truly the most enlightened of us, are those whose sensibilities are more tender and sensitive to the slightest glimpses of human suffering.

154

It is best and most wise to be silent at one's misfortunes, for in doing such with true thought of the weightiness of the matter, one may see for the first time the folly that is his very own.

155

Dare not mock or publicize the ill of another, for the least of mercy that you employed. Even lesser shall be shown unto you.

204

Wisdom is seldom spoken but surprisingly is always there to be seen. However, many never display it, yet in one who is wise about learning one's own self, therein lies one's ability to recognize it, once it appears.

203

The forming of any man's character is determined by his perceptions, one's stature is no greater or lesser than such.

134

Truth is really a phenomenon, for being in pursuit of it, the greatest power of mobilization that can inspire the human

being is unleashed, which
simultaneously brings about the
actualization of one's own potential.

152
Through the late night hours protruding
to the brightening morning, between
such there are for any contemplative
spirit thunderous moments filled with
flashing enlightening revelation for true
conscientious development to starry
wondrous ideas of ingenuity for man's
evolution.   It is a shame that such toiling
is not done more often.   Then I dare to
say that by dawn, the autonomy of a new
mind has start to form. Thereby such
laboring to this state of achievement, rest
becomes a sweet reward. Therein you
will find sweeter dreams, upon
awakening, the world appears new, not
in its activities, yet new as in how you
view it and as you involve yourself in it.

109

If any human, will dare to turn his
thoughts over daily, likened unto
reading a captivating story as in a book,
he will behold then a conversation
never known to oneself before. The
travesty of what he will discover in its
unadulterated language will probably
leave him spell bound. He will not
know how to proceed or what to make of
it, at such earth shattering moments,
though he will be contented to have
conceived such. I say perceive such, yet
for this (miner), he will thus have
learned that only in digging to such
purport man's discovered (awareness) is
what lurks beneath him, and is what now
has been made known. For the time
being nothing else matters.
Enlightenment then leads to one's own
self-discovery

199

The true sage is one who knows that a virtue, misappropriate, can easily become a vice. At any moment a vice can become a virtue if set proper in one's application and set proper in one's intent. Wisdom is more about seeing the submerged subtleties in one's actions, which gives man's actions its moral distinction, rather than just distinguishing if the act is overtly right or wrong.

90

Enlightenment is clearly the truth that you have essentially known, that has existed within ourselves, all along, becoming more crystallized day by day intricate details upon details.

Spiritualism/Philosophy

110

There is in every field of science, a
revelation of God that awaits man.

201

Life, is a journey, with many
beginnings! Each beginning will show
you having greater or lesser
understanding of its course.

81

To know true bliss, the standard of truth
in which one is striving towards, must be
met consistently. If not, the
contentment of the mind will always be
constantly in want.
There is no self-discovery without self-
inquiry, for the actualization of one's
own potential. One must seek before he
finds; one cannot search without asking
the right questions in order to have the
right beginning in hope of discovering
the right ending.

198

I imagine every soul is born with two major conflicting inquiries. Both presents a sort of paradox…
The first inquiry being , "Who am I?"
Though interesting enough already believing that he indeed is somebody of much significance.

The second inquiry being, "Who is the ultimate caused behind my existence".
Yet possessing some premonition that one already knows and even more what He may require of him.
Therefore all the real answers of life is merely seeking to reconcile in some form these two great inquires.

199

The great charge of life is to make life worth living.

200

A dry soul is one uninspired by life and
the beauty it naturally possess;
uninspired by the reality that he has it
with its seemingly limitless possibilities.
and even more that he has the power to
give the very inspiration he lacks to
others.
May he then discover that most inspired
people find real inspiration in their lives
when uncovering the truth that what they
do with their lives has significant
influence upon what someone may do
with their own.

201

Inspiration is borne out of creativity,
creativity is borne out of life
experiences, and life experiences more
times than not are unforeseeable realities
being thrust upon us or already some
pre-existing circumstances having sway
over our little world .

But there in such a small space creativity is emerging, creating through self-expression a hole by which we can emerge leading into a light of day that never was before.

202

Inspiration is a major link between who you are today and who you are tomorrow. A major link connected to other essential links necessary for the forming of any masterpiece. But one must know that inspiration is more than an inciting feeling or grandiose idea that motivates ... it's actually an inner trait that the soul possess whenever the human being needs stimulation for perfecting, maturing, or developing anything that's of any noteworthy consequence.

None better than one's own character.

203

As a prisoner I have learned about being inspired from birds.
None more dearer than watching a bird reaching the highest fence of the compound and begin singing and suddenly flying away.
Two things I learned...
It matters not if you understand fully who, how, and why this song of life got pick, but it's totally up to you how you Sing it.
Secondly, the height of the prisoner cage isn't just a sign of his potential danger but just as well his capacity to rise above any form of degradation in which he may find himself.

204

Hear that... Is that You, that voice going off in your head, is that the Great Conscience, or is it Someone's else voice, it sounds like You, does it...do you know what to do with it, have you determine why it says, what does, if you can determine these things then the power of inspiration is yours for the keeping and the world in which it leads is really upon your own making. For whoever can determine the Great Voice within have discover the Author of all inspiration.

205

Behind the eyelids of every human being live the power of imagination, and in the realm of imagination lives a king named Inspiration. And in his hand is a ruling scepter called Faith and upon his head is crown called wisdom and upon his throne he sit's, made out iron covered in flawless gold called discipline and determination.

Summon this King, and victory is yours.

206

The real measure of anyone influence is found in the inspiration he provides not in the lives of those who knew him while alive but those who will come to know of him while dead. It is upon these individuals in which his influence will have the greatest impact.

Chapter 4

Torchlight

"You are extremely stubborn and defiant. You cannot continuously buck authority. You must learn to comply son. Rules and regulation are a part of life."

"But Mom, if it's unjust and not right, why should I? Even God doesn't command such a thing!"

"Jason, you are just rebellious and hard-headed that's all."

-Ghazzali's Mother

The exact laws of nature unceasingly permeates throughout our universe. Through much probing there's still so much more to discover and understand. This life naturally commands and compels us to learn them and what is to be our harmonious relation to them for our maintenance and advancement. This commanding impulse to learn the exact laws of our creation isn't just in regards to the universe yet in regards to this phenomenon known as humanity! I believe those who remain ignorant such exacting laws that pervades through all the human race with all its subtleties will continuously bear the burden of major consequences from choices that are not their own... Be careful of the ignorance you choose to embrace!

Knowledge

36

The first and only cry in which the human ever truly give sound to is the cry for understanding!

37

Understanding is knowledge well-experienced, embraced, and shared.

35

What distinguishes the cry of the boy from that of the maturing man? The cry of the boy desires to know "WHAT IT IS", the cry of the man is to know "WHY IT IS - WHAT IT IS", One is curiosity, the other is responsibility!

34

One may ask what form of knowledge is best to be pursued? Simply, the form of knowledge that knows no shape!

31

For all our aims or reasons in 'knowing'
when finally crossing the threshold of
execution, the purposeful pleasure of
knowledge yields a joy without end.

30

Once the passionate pursuit of
knowledge is truly ignited, the mind's
intrigue senses no restraint on its ability
to grasp and hold its beautifying
wonders! Only the thinker in question
will be left awe-stricken.

32

There are two storehouses for the
housing of knowledge ... The storehouse
for today and storehouse for tomorrow.
The storehouse for today is where we
draw from for our daily maintenance and
survival. The storehouse for tomorrow
is where we expect to draw from for our

future expectations and betterment ...
Both storehouses commands the best of
our efforts having bountiful surplus for
supply and demand.

33

Beware of false pursuers of this
immaculate gift called knowledge, for
it's empowering of saints is less known
than what we have witnessed of the
forming of many devils. Pursuers that
are false have obtained much by it
(knowledge) but have known very little
or none at all of the service to be
rendered to others by way of it
(knowledge)!

Success

104

Men who are notably successful and
greatly envied by others are so. Not
because of their achievements, but due

to the unconventional means by which it was attained.

144

The real success of any noble conquest isn't any reaching the 'top of the hill' but knowing what you're going to build to stay there.

165

Success is impossible without a solid work ethic, but discovering an ethic that 'works' is the key to a successful life.

179

He who dares to dream 'Big Dreams' without becoming them every day has created the quicksand for his own failure!

169

In the giant quest for great success people can be more powerful, intelligent, charismatic and even richer than you but working harder than you is totally optional.

Family

94

Powerful families are truly the real pillars of any and every society, influencing the human personalities in the most dominant positions or they themselves are in one, shaping the great institutes and structures that are holding proactive sway of our world. Even if such families become immoral in their dealing throughout generations they are still able to secretly illicit in us, a sense of deep regard and admiration.

93

Critically understood must be that a man's family and its tedious construction is his best, primary, scrupulous and most satisfying labor.

To fail here without exception is to lose a vital voice in one's assertion of his masculinity; by which hearing him any further becomes extremely difficult.

92

Family is more than a collection of persons tied by a common bloodline ... It's society's most dignified institution filled to immerse everyone of its members, even in its most early years to the understanding of identified roles, inherent responsibility, learning how to be a team player and contributing to the benefit of the whole. Therefore, through rigorous training, by love and discipline, allowing the human being to emerge with an understanding of its role and responsibility to the larger society known as the world.

95

The prized possession of family virtues, among any family, is loyalty! This principle virtue provides one of the most fertile grounds from which all success, productivity, and collaborative growth can be achieved. Family loyalty is its demonstrative love of commitment for one another being found unbroken, unquestioned, unrelenting, and most indestructible. The family whose crown wears such a jewel reigns as long the name remains among the land of the living!

Leadership

72

Every leader should be structured and organized to give greater efficiency to one's objectives. For requirements such as these isn't only for rightness of actions but the right usage of time and space.

46

Any leader that takes on the personal challenge of primarily being the principal educator of his people, must have a regardful and acute understanding for their intellectual attitude, aptitude, and appetite'

59

A leader should be firm in proven, unshakable principles, yet flexible in measuring the discretion that should be shown in taking tactful approaches when addressing issues that are similar requiring different solutions.

23

The enormous task of raising consciousness comes with strenuous pressure and calls for great patient precision likened unto a skilled physician. For our earnest laborers, who toils for the well-being of others,

the warrior image is truly overplayed!
For in my own modest toiling, I have
seen the scalpel of truth more called for
than the sword!

80

One cannot assume to be an educator of
any until first a rigorous learning is
pursued towards the undisciplined areas
of one's own mind!

117

All authentic leadership is dutifully
entitled to its rightful share, the rationing
out of harsh criticism, unjust ridicule,
false accusations, duplicitous judgments,
and envious slander! Every leader in
such times must find a way to keep a
resplendent resolve for wise construction
and true development of its people;
proving himself to be all the more
sincere, true, and steadfast... For the
nobility ascribe to the calling itself and
demand such of him.

125

Beware, anytime a leader is forced to
give evidence to his brute power, under
girding his position, even for goodness
sake; the people will be sharply
reminded as well the potentiality of that
same power can equally cause
unrelenting harm.

130

Leaders of unparalleled stature are never
followed in their lifetime the way they
are followed almost (god-like) in the
event of their demise.

168

Leadership and its development: If a
man is highly eager to lead, avoid him.
If a man's aim is only to follow
watch him.
If a man is of honest indecisiveness, then
show him.

If a man is neutral just because, stay away from him.
If any of these men are you, then, make ready for war.
If any man says none of these are him... then the bed of self-delusion is its own grave.

173

Leadership is a living dynamic to the natural order of life. It is not a preferring of one above another, but more of life perfecting its arrangement on the necessary progression of human affairs by affording responsibilities to those endowed with distinctive dispositions and capabilities.

174

The lighted messages found in divine leadership known as prophet-hood stands guiding global communities for all time! Moses' message is to any oppressed people, that the flight of their exodus to their believed promise land of freedom must not only be a guided one, yet it should lead in establishing for that freedom a divine law! Jesus' lighted message is clearly that only divine love is inherently sacrificial, and therefore purely redemptive ...Yet Muhammad's lighted message towards the west is our global challenge of today; and that is Law, balanced with Love can only provide and pave the way for true peace and justice ...

27

The greatest demand upon any leader in regards to the sacred trust that exist between him and his people is to model first what he will impart in them as principles to live by.

115

After long stressful seasons of public
service it is best at times for any leader
to schedule moments of lengthy periods
of reclusion. Sometimes dependent on
the post - permanent resignation. The
leader should return back to the place in
which any real leader has emerged that
being the intense private affairs of
studying his most cherished disciplines
and perfecting his love for its core
essential! Here, he enjoys the eye of his
most vital critic ...(Himself).

77

A weight of insurmountable stress, not
fitted for any one member to carry upon
his or her shoulders, within any society,
organization, or institution is to witness
one's own leadership warring with one
another.

126

The best of naturally-gifted leaders,
notably unmatched in abilities, and in
strategically wielding influence, abhors
so-called designated positions or post of
authority that seemingly restricts their
movements or anything that seeks to
assign them to one targeted area and
which marginalizes their dominant
strengths. For this unique class of men,
this appears to be some sort of
imprisonment and deadens the vitality of
their spirits. They will seek to revolt,
eventually, liberating themselves in all
matters true to their innate creativeness
having no concerns for whatever
traditional boundaries, restrictions, or
prohibitions that have been set
in place. This spirit lives among any
dispensation of mankind yet few
personalities have shown to possess such
a spirit in these modern times.

207

The world suffers today not from a lack of committed soldiers but from a lack of generals with noteworthy causes.

208

The wisdom that should accompany any leader best for the people he attends to serve is best found among those who has suffer the most from its rejection or ignorance.

209

The spirit of taking the initiative is usually found in the souls most dissatisfied with being subjected to circumstances of life engineered by the hands of others and not their own.

210

Who wants a compass, when there is a guide? Better to have an experience traveler than to be left to one's wits ends… A head full speculative ideas.

211

The greatest dilemma plaguing Uncle Sam's society is convincing the American youth that life isn't one great big party and the world isn't going to forever dance to it's music. Better latter than never; America needs to hastily busy herself with the business of giving birth to new sons and daughters.

212

Beware of the drunken optimism of materialism: for the beginning decline of many great empires was when they were at the height of their wealth and their lives was filled with every luxurious and pleasurable thing known to man. Yet under drunken material consumption they was latter sober up by erosion from with under, invasion from without, and perversion from within.

213

The new modem leaders of today aren't elected as the days of old: by way of whole tribes, nations, boards, committees, omens, angels, or something divine ... No I'm afraid you not keeping pace with the times; in this age to come leaders are elected by the conditions of life themselves in which they have been most affected or those they love or their peers or the human family as a whole. Their appointment is strictly basis on them perceiving such conditions unbefitting of the human being inherited dignity or esteem character.

214

The new age of progression will not emerge from the distinguishable families of the powerful and the rich. Neither from the great ivy league schools, military academy, the silicon valleys of the world, or new political party. But due to the world moving towards social globalization, the new light of progression will come from the most remotest places in the earth, and it will not come with any new tech software, new medicine, new arms of war, or any new age religion or philosophy. But a new consciousness that's most basic to our human nature: a moral conscious and pure reasoning basis on justice, equity, and love.

215

A leader typically does three things exceptionally well: describe what sees, explain how to get there, and lead the way.

Chapter 5

Footprints

"Jason, what we are doing today will impact and effect us tomorrow. I mean much later down the road, your mom is seeking to leave sort of legacy for our family to inherit. Something to be enjoyed by, not only you all (as my sons), my grandchildren, when they come, and their own children. But can you all be trusted with such; as of right now it will be ruined before I'm placed in the grave. Your character and conduct improving , is the only thing that makes you trustworthy".

-Ghazzali's Mother

Most men struggle to learn how to live only to die, while very few struggle to learn how to die, in order to finally live.

Commendable Qualities

12

The task of dignity is in all things to keep the highest regard for one's self and others without compromising or contradicting either

25

The simple question always is ... when it comes to integrity; "Can you trust yourself when alone?"

133

The art of speaking isn't merely putting thoughts into one's head, but converting those thoughts into colorful images in the mind's eye.

157

We must not be false to each other; we must develop the heart of truthfulness to speak honestly about our hurts, defeats, and imperfections.   Here ... in our struggling, humanity being laid bare, all the elements needed for collective unity can be shaped and form.

136

Union: The two become one; is an eternal process not really about man and woman, but the story is really about God, man, the world, and destiny.

132

With every new dawn let it awaken in us an awareness that is brighter than the day before.

161

Let not last night's failures lead to early morning disgraces.

189

In the height of one's most triumphant moment, the arrogance which one should withstand makes itself known while in the state of one's defeat the humility that one needs in order to enjoy life's greatest successes will also become most evident. How well can anyone see themselves in these vital moments?

89

Man's ways that lead to destruction are endless and our world's glooming demise seems alarmingly inevitable. It's the down spiraling effect that's seemingly taking us with it that seems so undeniable as well. Unless, there is within you an internal fortitude to withstand its tempestuous ways, by having the capacity to withdraw oneself or retire to a whole 'otherly' world that is just as lively... where man becomes his own best moralistic critic. As self-judge weighing, analyzing, the nature of his thoughts, testing the performance of his deeds with resolve to reconstruct a character truly fitting to an image, identity, in which he desires the world to be.

129

All servants who labor in the cause of their spiritual lord or master must never bemoan what he thinks is his unjust suffering ... Yet his spiritual master knows that what he bemoans is essential for the depth of his service to become most pure, selfless, and

sacrificial.   But the servant himself will
learn that even these affronts or assaults are
truly not directly towards him but belong to
his master as well. ...

97

The artful weapon of diplomacy is
essentially skillful negotiating; negotiations
are a tester of one's resolved and patience,
then patience behooves us to weigh
thoroughly our proposed objectives,
agendas, and solutions, to never falsify our
proposals by what is actually true in our
hearts.

84

The blooming of greatness doesn't always
appear in some grandiose form or way. Yet
it comes slowly in sparkling increments;
connecting one revealing moment to the
next! Remain steadfast; even if the span
thereof is many years apart.

22

Mercy accompanies the ignorant often for their ignorance is by way of innocence; but with the willful ignorant justice will demands it rightful retribution

52

The aftermath of participating in fierce dialogue with men of power, debating over feverish appeals is to witness an animation out of the human spirit that when all voices have fallen silent, tongues have gone parched, and minds gone blank with nothingness, either we sense we have cheapened our own human dignity or we have reached inside of us, the most angelic side of our nature.

75

To be passionless in one's profession is to convey a sense of irrelevancy not to the trade or field in of itself but unfortunately to those whom it intends to benefit.

145

A display of insolence is shown to the integrity of any political process; when executing judicial procedures for a massive call for justice, 'merciful' partiality is thus shown.

176

The Best of recommendations: Be great,
Be productive, Command excellence in all
you do, Know thy self, Seek wisdom
Live above your conditions,
Always seek to be just, and love
righteousness even when it hurts
Cherish your parents even though they are
flawed,
Always show your 'sons' the best of
manhood, place no limit upon their hearts,
minds; and abilities. Learn to love woman

for the sake of her unfading beauty: That of
righteousness,
A mind of intelligent grace,
Her sway of elegance and hidden romance
Hopefully who lives for God and family
above all things.

For lust blinds, love makes all things clear
eventually Lust encourages and craves
exploitation, love teaches us to serve and
empowers us to be serviceable, yielding to
one another... without concern of misuse .
At last worship and trust God, love self
always in truth, and restore the best of
mankind: in these three there have never
been found any lack thereof.

217

Men typically wage three types of wars: war
with self, war with the world, and war with
God: only in the war with self , if he wins,
will he become the victor of the other two.

218

The sharpest tools in the toolbox for the
construction of our world is the human
mind and the organ of the tongue yet the
level of maturity of the human heart will
determine if we preparing to build for better
world or merely working to be destroyed.

219

The marvelous truth regarding divine
guidance is that it naturally corresponds to
innate road map written on the human soul,
so then wherever divine guidance is
ultimately leading us our souls naturally
aspires to be.

220

The most exemplary men and women have
the profound ability to absorb up meaningful
space in our lives, making that time feel

most momentous and leaving us with the feeling we on the verge of becoming better than we once were because we have spent time in their presence.

221

Somewhere is some unthinkable place in the world there is an obscure, yet unique personality coming forth with an invention that will bring his little space and the world to a great colliding, be it may that you will be there to witness, to partake, or be beneficiary or even the benefactor itself. Nevertheless this world has yet to cease from fashioning or molding its greatest product: that is great minds.

222

The curse of today is that it has no thought of tomorrow, and the benefit of tomorrow is that enjoy the spoils of today, and the harsh reality of today is must bear the burden of yesterday. Wise is he who masters his days and having consideration for what will become yesterday, what will be today, and what shall be tomorrow.

223

The beauty of every deed is not found in anything that can be witness external, but internally where the soul remains untainted by any guilt or dissatisfaction with oneself

224

No joy is greater than finding truth of life, purpose, and one's calling. Everything else shall pass in time.

225

Destiny is the eternal union between purpose and character.

226

Your best friend in life is the person who can enjoy who you are at the height of your success and love who you are not when you at your lowest.

If you are here reading this page you have made the journey through a chronicle of significant sayings, lessons, and critical principles that have been etched somewhere deep within the bosom of my very own heart

I pray that you have glean something meaningful and note -worthy enough in your eyes to help aid you in your own personal journey. We (humans), indeed stay in constant need of encouragement, inspiration, and timeless remainders for navigating through life's terrain when we become most prone to fear, doubt, anxiety, despair, and sorts of hopelessness. In all of our quest to find purpose, meaning, and much needed significance. Many of these quotes just naturally formed themselves out of mere observation of watching so many sons of incarceration fight to spiritually, mentally, and morally find their way.

Growth behind concrete walls is a brutal task and an heart wrenching endeavor with practically no systematized assistance or vital educational structure that's relevant, modern in its approach, technologically based or universally broad enough to armed the few sincere ones with meaningful tools in their process of change. In terms of re organizing and reforming their shattered lives. So then we are forced to make due amongst ourselves, to pull resources from among ourselves, and more critically to cast our nets much more deeper within oursrleves.

To unearth those hidden gems invested in us by our Wonderful Creator that sheds more profound light on man's noble calling, destiny, and perfected character.

Often times these reverberating truths was
first echo in us deep by precious influences
within the fabric of our own lives.
For me specifically my mother!

I   pray whoever these memorable persons
may have been for you that you make good
on their investment, by walking in the light
of truth in which their wisdom represent.

I   pray you make good on their promise of
belief and hope in you by fulfilling your
highest potential, and make good on their
sacrifices made in honor of your awaited
destiny, and make good on their continuous
support in anticipation of seeing you walk
with dignity and independent of needing
others for self worth. Do give them the joy
and enthusiasm of being proud and seeing
their wisdom come to full fruition.

Nothing compares to a gratitude of love such as this. To my own bless mother my this book be the first installment in me simply saying Thanks.

Author, Ghazzali

Special Acknowledgements:

Truly all thanks belongs to our Most Merciful Creator and Redeemer... Allah ta'ala(The Most High). For it is by Him alone do we have the power to inspire, to envision, and to become.

I give thanks to my dear mother for being the full inspiration behind this book and surely her work in my life goes on without end.
Hail to the Queen ... all smiles!
May you receive great joy from this accomplishment.

Also much love to the Kimble clan as a whole. Special thanks for your support through some very difficult years.

To the Leal family, you all will always hold dear place within my heart ... Abel, what an incredible friend you have been, and may you forever remain so!

To all my fellow comrades, solders, brethren in the struggle much love always.

The T.U. family and the Coffield unit, words to the wise ... Simply make our naysayers a lie!

Special regards to a few exceptional men who have shown me personal unwavering loyalty, I love you dearly ....
A.C(Avery Cooke). Hafiz.the Hawk. King Tut. Loco Nate. The Great. Young Akbar, Shaky Hakim(Ranks Instructor), Imam Jamal, Jalib Ghalib, Big Talib, and Young Islam Imam Darweshi.

Definitely must mention my publisher and brother who rescued this body of work from the dungeon.

(Supreme). Mr.Reed may we shine a little brighter because of you!

To my dear brother and friend Randy George endless appreciation for your contribution to the Forward section of the book ..
You are a great mind and excellent teacher! Recall many joyous moments; you. Krote, and myself.

Lastly , to the most adorable woman I ever meet my wife Shifna.. No words can describe your presence in my life and it's enormous affect.
Beautiful indeed!
To you and your great and noble family ...
May Allah reward you of all greatly with the best in this life and the
Hereafter!

To my personal clan and squad of dear brothers... let's build and move with authority and due diligence. God willing! Peace

About the author:

Jason Kimble is an upcoming author and aspirant motivational speaker who has written his first book
Ghazzali's Treasure chest.

This is a 3 part book series called the Indelible Jewels series. Though currently serving a sentence within TD.C.J state prison Mr. Kimble has set his sight towards higher educational reform and being a instrumental voice in addressing the many social crisis plaguing our youth all across America such as mass incarceration and the lack of authentic manhood to a name a few.

Mr. Kimble better known as (Ghazzali) has earned a certification in Computer Information Technology through Trinity Valley Community College and is now pursing an Associate Degree in Applied Science

(Photos)
Top: Shifna – Ghazzali's wife
Bottom: Ghazzali's mother – Queen
Victoria

Published by
Ronnie Reed
A.R.D. Publishing
P.O. Box 850961
Mesquite, TX 75185

Peace

And

Blessings

www.ingramcontent.com/pod-product-compliance
Lightning Source LLC
La Vergne TN
LVHW021357080426
835508LV00020B/2326